Tripping Over Clouds

LUCY BURNETT is from south-west Scotland, and in recent years has been based in the north of England. She currently lives in Cockermouth, where she gets out in the fells at every opportunity, and works as Senior Lecturer in Creative Writing at the University of Cumbria. Previously she has worked at Leeds Beckett, Salford and Strathclyde Universities, and before that as an environmental campaigner for organisations including Ramblers Scotland and Friends of the Earth. Apart from writing and academia, she is a photographer, a keen fellrunner and recently completed climbing the Scottish Munros. Her website can be found at: www.lucyburnett.net.

T0158636

Also by Lucy Burnett

Leaf Graffiti (Carcanet / Northern House 2013)
Through the Weather Glass (Knives Forks and Spoons Press 2015)

LUCY BURNETT

Tripping Over Clouds

C A R C A N E T • Northern House

First published in Great Britain in 2019 by
Northern House
In association with Carcanet Press Ltd
Alliance House, 30 Cross Street
Manchester M2 7AQ
www.carcanet.co.uk

A CIP catalogue record for this book is available from the British Library.
ISBN 978 1 784107 43 7

The publisher acknowledges financial assistance from Arts Council England.

Supported by
ARTS COUNCIL
ENGLAND

Typeset in England by XL Publishing Services, Exmouth
Printed and bound in England by SRP Ltd, Exeter

For Anna

Contents

III

IV

Tripping over clouds

all things hoping
all things being just so and so

if you could name a colour
which colour and what and these
days' lumber is behind us and how

    for several weeks now

        pavements greying
beneath my feet cracks opening me
as cloud racks tumble over sky
in the pure dead edge of:

there's something not quite right
about the colour of daffodils

    but I may yet not
    remember these times

    friday mornings
    tripping over clouds

so in whatever colour you might come
and avoiding cracks in pavements and
collecting clouds and if I were
transparent as sunshine might I smile

I

or is this day a day this mountain and the ways of wind against air
and the time of did you love the moment or did you ever choose to
love the moment you see me dare to hope the best to touch of solid
air and until further then to mountain

Big Sands

The grains were small as the storm
had thrown them
– over – and I was waiting
for the weather and strong legs
to return me to a mountain-
version of myself
that the years had carried elsewhere.

Can you hear the rustling of grasses
and the cries of crooked-angled gulls
as they unbecome the wind
and the individual storms in-fighting
for their portion of morning?

This is a not a day for the beach
but of the seashore.

The sand makes gritted seaweed
from my hair as an elongated snail
traverses machair to a predetermined
nowhere. Wagtails line the roof of a boarded hut
while a kite spears the clouds like an inverse
sunbeam; a tern nibbles the edges of some
barbecued wood and the tumbled laundry
of a down-day is crafting the motions of
a 'pound for fourteen minutes' of waves.

This is a place of uncalled-for space
and by the grace of the big sky,
and the serrated under-silhouette of Skye,
an invitation to the sea unfolds
to come and dine with mountain.

The fellrunner

to talk about
the pleasure principle
of falling downhill fastly

I agree with running
      mainly

            the condition of mud
            as controlled slippage

      feet dancing
      to the score of impulse
      dripping rainbows from my smile

            my innocence
implies
a headlong gravity:

      mountain
      heartbeats failing
      drowning saltwater

            I sometimes even think

      how little
      death might be

          but barely

                foot-studs
stopping-up
the past participle   to fall

Brig-hills

Brag
before brig
and the hillsides flatten you

        each its part apart
from our slow slow-way –
we chased our shadows into mist
and danced away the final gravities –

        down the furrowed
foreheads of ancestral pathways –
ancient droves the cows had cut
to slipping gutturals

        each pelt of rain unseaming
        seems of early autumn.

To speak of
nature – then – would have been
to ridicule such clarity of body and the
pain-paving descant of the fells

        the runners are fledged
        cattle bellow
        the fells improvise their own decay.

Our lines were memorised
(muddied and returned   forgotten)

        such hurdling sway
    to brag before whose vowels flattening.

Pendle

from the cumbric word
'pen' meaning hill or head

I did not dream
euphoria of hillsong
failing nothing but

if the heart might
stop a moment
like a photograph

my questions wore
the hillside
from the poem
and this pulse of pen

a hill a head

the passage
of our feet eroding
moments:

if my failures
were a kind of memory
I put my heart into

Dunmail Raise

wait awhile not yet not yet the morning these herdwick bone-broke heathers chill to the wind where my seat is but a sandal to the sky now drops to water take this mountain mind one eye-step further to the climb the curve of shoulder nethermost and opening upon such *yellowness:* dun moorland edges at the cliff-raise *wake* the caw of dunmail – thermals crowning contours rising early leave displacement touches on a summit cross-cairn and the crow-stole day

I purchased wisdom

from the strands of moorland
grasses brushing up against
my forehead at the someplace
where we lost the wind

the blue sky opened to
butterflies and wildflowers
and the sunshine cuffed my shoulder
where my body met my skin

this blade of grass this bone
an imprint of a moorland
and the moorbirds calling still
this solitary moment not alone

this blade of bone this grass
this calling into stone
and still this sometime sometime
where the grasses grasses will

Stoodley Pike

There is no measurement
of mist as long as my imagination
continues emptying –

        we swam the
unbounded edges of the
common moor

      (no beginnings nor endings
woken from the mist)

          everything we could
not see contained the weight of water

      built
      before
      our eyes

      an obelisk
      of disappearance

      drawing weather
      from stone

      (now you can
      see through me
      now you don't – the sublimity
      of translucent bone)

I cannot extend to you much further
than this memory
withheld within
the hollow monumental shell of things

Shepherd's Skyline

spared length tributaries –
sharp passage

    a spine's brain offering of long miles
spilling the fast of the dipping hill's horizon
to my corporeal quick

        to speak of skin and muscles
        and the address of isolated limbs –

            I wore the speed
            of the shepherd's skyline like sciatic fell

            posterior chains
            of falling exhilaration
                    a multiplicity of erosions
            and the metallic taste of lactic frost

to be alive is a free submission –
a reduced pain threshold of tomorrow always comes
and the foreground heartbeat travel
of the mud-bleak moorland smiles

Three things I love (and three things over)

I wish to speak
to you

of happiness
and many other little
things –

what's the collectivity
of that much smile?

the faraway springtime
fields the potential
monotony of

        against walls
        against clouds
        against the road end

or where cows masticate
the green green grass

        and if there's nothing funny
        about the shape of the wind

then what's *your* preferred
form of loss?

Bat-running

(the Calderdale Way)

we run out of the night sky with our brains slanted
holding fast to the acceleration of black earth
and the weather receding from our outheld grasp

when we hit the moor the speed of stones over-
whelms the grass in search of music

> *colder*
> > *calder*
> > > *calmer*

and while my compass undoes our instinct for direction
our headtorch beams lead onward down the paving
slabs of Pennine night –

there is no single word
to capture the sense of valley shadow-swimming

> (what if permission to continue becomes
> more interesting than permission to change?)

my fascination with a rusted barbed wire fence
has little to do
with constant corners moonlit cloud banks promises of rain

Newlands

I ate the valley
that tried to get away

I was already running
late but it had this look
about it

so juicy green

you asked
if we could drink
a gluttony of sun

and fuck tomorrow
as if we
literally meant it

the valley
had this look about it
that took my guts away

we built ourselves a home
from bone nests
and we ate that too

Crow Hills

barely space
for namesakes
between driving weather

two crows' unconscious
recollections fall into reflection
of displaced memory:

> *the encephalisation quotient of a moorland outlives the future of*
> *sexual dimorphism which gathers in large communal roosts of*
> *intelligence – and if you can still differentiate then murder is not*
> *monogamous – how wonderful!*

the omnivorous
moorlands joust with dense
fossil omens

– two hills two hills –
amidst the close proximity of others –

Flower Scar

of what there is but
and the turbines cut the tussocks
of my eye and all this purity

adrenaline was shitting it

I'd willingly give my insides
to the flower
that scarred a mountain

(I even dreamt of stopping-
up the hillside with sky)

the peewits are like sugar-acid
burning through the bog-moss veins

and the eerie sibilance
of electric wind becoming

breath

I extended
my flower-scarred body to the moor
and ran with it

Marathon

after Nicolas de Staël

Harsh way
on the long concrete path –
the athletic equivalent
of stone-throwing.

The marathon runner's body
wore the echo of his physicality
in explosive fits and starts –
sinews of red green white
on a dull background beat of grey.

Muscles composed upon the reverse
of themselves – canvas on oil –
an anxiety of colour finding expression
in 26.3 long strokes of irregular emotion:

> *the runner wears the awkwardness*
of co-existence in an impasto of symbolic
gesture encoding meaning in convention
alised movements of please –
will you never take my hand?

The more I looked the less I seemed
to understand. The runner took
a palette knife to his prodigal return
and crafted his excess from it.

Fascia

Of course
it was always inevitable.

My inflamed tread on the mountain became
a torn connective tissue – bog tendons –
a ruptured insertion of nerve-bracken

yet still
the frontal lobes of rocks
lay still

      prone to abstraction –

(other worlds lie flat to
prevent the earth from running?)

          The mountain's eyes
          remained resilient
          as the passage of granite.

Sleep-standing

I have this to say
to knowledge

of the kind
that woke the horse

where it stood

      still
      sleeping

and realised that the day
had begun before it

      and if the dew
feels cold as diamonds
on the neck

      or your limbs
leaf-shortened as the trees

      then look!
      there still, the valley

         look! the sun

So much mountain

i. Lurg Mhor

beyond fear is a remote kind of
freshwater electricity
lacking comparative grandeur

      beyond the corrie of the fallow cattle
sharp slabs of moss slip through
the cliffs of the long ridge alone

this is the place of nameless rivulets
untrodden flanks of mountain antler
spine –

      the mist is lost inside itself
and while my blood tastes of mercury
my slightness
echoes in my ears like dam-shadows –

the future runs fast as closure
and the reservoir's blind eye

ii. Sgritheall

from screel to sgritheill
as a linguistic traverse of everything
I've ever loved from south to north

mountains wearing sky and purpling –
heather embodied in rising rock-water –
stones fall from my feet like I am shooting meteors

iii. A'Mhaighdean

you want names and I give you names –
the pure hard matter of them

I did not see a single person and the pinnacles fell into the sky like
stalactites and me out here alone with rocks for boots and the clouds
enclosing on me and I dare you to tell me that anything is not now
possible. A maiden is a mountain. My thoughts are stacked and
ruddy. The lochan is black and white and yesterday's rain already
sprouting from me.

Lochan

at the end of the
speed of sound

        where just
the early morning hum
of tree traffic
and mist-clothed hopes
of yet another day to come
and another yet gone –

heart as little exhibit
as a brain of cumulus
where forests strip
mountainsides of timber
long as cul de sacs

while steam inversions
of a world in negative
cause the largest stones to float –

a dream is a dream is –

not even yet a loch
that took the place
that was no place
at the end not yet a road and still
a kind of depth
we might have swum with it

II

Here I am, then. A table.
Coffee. I imagine your hand.

At

and on abstraction
I have this to –
love
as yellow a canvas

                    •

can you feel the way
we talk out lightness

            moss-grid cobbles
                    drystone lichen
                            a day at a

            layers of square / textured / sun
            hesitate to
            stone shade shadow or

            (such a thing as levity of and all this)

                    •

or simply – say
            a word a smile

morning deafening
spring with another kind of leap / tread /

                            yearning for
the absence of birds and the yellow lichen
brushstroke of opaque wind

I love nobody but

nobody loves pathos
more than the shredded plastic bag
impaled on the post
by the canal

the day's mood has already
exceeded its usefulness

        the lonely offering
        of an empty park bench
                rotting leaves

                    unsigned graffiti
        and a sluice gate scaffold
        emptying other afternoons of rain

I sit apart
and make
as if to wait –

for the long-anticipated gales
from way out east

on the place where nobodies and
words like but and sunsets grow

How doth the moon

where
little words but neatly
adapt old water
don the obsolete canvas / scale

       I once believed
       in my apprehension
       of dreams

       the meaning
       of bodies and tides
       and other, private matters –

a solitary woman
drifts to sea until the moon unravels
into orbits of itself

see the fish tails smiling
and the oarless boat
as our protagonist becomes a foil
for solar systems made of distant
night-times, doesn't matters and
the merest grasp of individual stars of snow –

Birdsong

so there you are then magpie, cycling along the road with your helmet tucked beneath one arm like a rugby ball and the cobbles throwing your smile from side to side as the streetlights compete with the dusk and your eyes dart this way / that as you dodge the cars the wrong way up a one-way street and despite the way I call so clearly out to you, I know you won't reply, because I can barely even bring to mind the sound of birdsong

Lavender Mist

after Jackson Pollock

V. I

So I *did* the lavender
and became of mist
and by the time that I returned home
the only thing that was left of me
was my headache – and a small vial
easily misplaced – of concentrated flower.
No matter how I scrubbed I could not
remove the perfume from my nose.

V.2

I was hauntingly clear as blue-green foliage
along matte stems and my sprays of nodding lilac
flowers had yellow stamens. I earnt my place
in the world through my foliage alone
but I also do quite well as a backdrop
or as a see-through person in mixed company.

That was the day I realised that I was not yet in love
and it was time to keep on journeying –
after all, the world cannot be grasped in a single glance
and my rapport with it was not yet final.

I come from the active passage of pure abstraction.
Powdery mildew, rust, white smut and leaf spots, slugs.

We begin again

a spider climbs the trellis of its web
wearing the inside of every circle out

(I've often wondered about the texture
of slippage – no dust settles on dusk)

to become survives a form of epithet –

> *imagine* a tree with no horizon
> stars without darkness
> tiredness waking morning from insomnia
>
> I've heard it said that inhabiting
> a locked white cell for any length of time
> resembles death and I believe it

the sun pulls back its muslin skin
and the spider keeps on climbing
as if there's simply no way else to go

innocence does not possess the quality
of diffracted light
and my lack of apology for my limitations
becomes the condition for
everything that has come before

The incremental lightness of love

a lightness
of touch
conditional

if love

a kind of time

accelerating
abstraction   attraction

we run grey sand
up through our fingers

i love
you love
she loves

an indirect weight
rising from greyscale earth

Gibbous moon

you take my hand
as if a touch so
unfrequented

or of knowledge
(merely talking)

and perhaps of
many other little things

you became from
debris-falling slowly
and the matter of rain

an opacity
to share
a likelihood
accumulating

you are the loss
i choose to gain?

the etymology
of moments from
momentum shifts

(the density of time)

a darkness weighing
light of textures air
to touch *become*

shared waning
of a gibbous moon on
pale-cloud blue of morning

The narrow handle

The dark oval mouth of the wine carafe
inhales the air of a lazy Sunday evening
as if its being depends on it.

       I can even taste you
       from this distance as I trace
       the narrow convex terracotta curve
       of the carafe's inner neck.

Solitude has this way
about it that undoes the knotted pattern
of the Merlot's veins,
transporting the vineyard
from the mountains to the river
to the mouth of our greedy seas.

       I hide from the all-seeing gaze
       of the setting sun
       as if there is some truth in it.

My wine's blood is alive
and reducing me –
take the handle of this terracotta
jug and lay me on the table –
it is evening – and we must realise.

I've learnt the knotted path
of the long vine
and the time to drink has years to come.

Sacking and Red

after Alberto Burri

Please don't touch the paintings
because the sacking chafes
and the backdrop burns.

The wheatfields were scattered with
random bales and roofless barns.
I could not even conceive of the size
of the sky as I took your roughened hand
in mine, and we stopped awhile.

Beneath the sacking of the surrounding
landscape lay the contours
of your naked sleeping body.
Ground pumice and kaolin, tutu netting
and PVC glue. Torched charred bleeding.

I saw beauty and that was all.

The sun pricked my skin through
the open car window, and I said, 'I love you,
you know.' You smelt of melted
tar and your kiss had the taste of burnt metal.

Girl with a basket of fruit

drawing angles off texture
     a slight of shadow tilted
towards an upraised expectation

       alight?
           if so

you ask
about still life
as if another possibility exists
     comparisons deadened through indulgent nature

I have no wondrous shadows
     (the mirror of a doubt)

          expectation is a girl
with an empty basket of fruit and more so

Sunset, revisited

Now, right this second
I am once more standing
on my hands and staring
at the middle of the sunset
from the inside out
and it feels kind of *normal* here.

As if I've been here
– only once perhaps – before.

If you were here as well
you'd tell me that the sky
is bleeding and the sun's no longer
true and that there's something
tragic and yet timeless about
the white line in the middle
of the sunset that's disturbing you.

But I'm sorry.
I'd be far too busy balancing
upon my hands
to truly listen to you.

The infinity of nothing

if all things were only not
then infinite both in number
and by rule

or a kind of smallness mixed
for the small too would be alone

and the infinite would be itself
and by itself and in turn

·

I group the noughts and crosses
in opposing corners of the sheet

what's the opposite of emotion?

I light the fire
I don't like winter
night is the opposite of light

extreme withdrawal –

the first nought takes my mood
and encloses me in it

I watch the fire empty itself
across is a cross with

it is winter

darkness is not the opposite of light

Untitled

after Mark Rothko

silence is so accurate
that I find myself
obliged to ask

if we'd listened to
the silence then

but all of this
and rather – differently

whether silence is white
whether white is possible

whether possibility took the open
space of sunlight out of doors –
to listen to it

The Poetess

after Joan Miró

But of the poetess
you will find her
here and there and everywhere.

There have been poetic stars.
There has been every kind of moon.
On one occasion I had thought the painting
of the poet had a nose but it turned out
just to be a double-headed bird
and I didn't choose to seek an explanation.

Poems don't contain solutions
any more than cave paintings
contain non-sequiturs.

To conclude. Do you still remember that
I love you? I'm looking at you from the corner
of my eye while you're pretending to be reading
about the history of women's art.

It's long since been on trend to turn your eyes
into an I, and spreading, and here's the evidence –

the world has been all over me.
But then again, the world and love and loss
have been all over.

Sticks

your centre carried
where other muscles couldn't
or just can't keep up or just can't –
winter blew the wind from your face

> you were here once before
> and did not remember me

the turn of year will have a kind of violence
to it – anger pooling off to the right and not
quite centre – we will find you

Seeing Round Corners

Margate, 3 September 2016

Seeing round corners – brains spinning around the extended stalks of our dislocated eyes abroad the underside of the sun's fast circle. The trick is seeing your own reflection in the convex of your contact lenses? (We tried to be caricatures of someone else but got it wrong and who did that make us?) At the centre of the circle was the ellipsis of the idea of a circle, as if the immediate prospect of the future flattened us. Plane-struck skies and a yellowing chromatic wash of sea and the apple trees the apple trees – the apple trees were not for turning.

A near-continuous accumulation

i.

If the overall idea
behind fake flowers
is eternal life then

the runnels on my face
are already crusted with dust
and the sea is lowing

and the lilies have delivered
their own souls to the sky
and all of this and this unless
the sun?

                      The clock
has forgotten how to bother
and the seagulls look – somehow –
baggier with every passing moment.

Natural languages are ambiguous
and I was born with this dread
of indoor water – breaking –

an adequate sufficiency or the title
of the question is necessarily mistaken.

ii.

Rainfall
as a state of full doubtfulness
and yet still falling / failing:

the difference between the future
and the palm of your hand is merely
in it?

The precipitation lacked
precise diameter
where the sky wanted for wings

and I remembered how you'd said you'd
called as I crossed the concrete pavement
to the tarmac road and thought how

       to fail is uncommon
       to or
       to define otherwise

       and how rain rises vertically
       on a calm day and if only I could read
       the easy slippage
       of its shopfront window-lines –

fate through head to heart to life
(or simply fifty different words for rain).

If you were to offer me your hand
I would complete it
with a state of doubtfulness still full to falling.

iii.

So you told me it was once more
morning / raining (hard not to think of
mourning sometimes) and did I want another
coffee and I didn't need to answer that.

Instead I explained how I'd come
to realise that knowledge is already
not allowed nor disallowed but rather –
more so.

We slurped our coffees and listened to
the sibilance of our resultant silence:
a kind of half-alive and half less-so.

If in the beginning was the word then
the word was *was* and that's the sum of it?

We liked coffee, and we had both been
indoor water-broken and these were things
we seemed – more or less –
to share with –

iv.

to lose the or the not at all:
how the fake flowers swayed to the rhythm
of the central heating breeze
and my headache lowed for the absence
of the sea and the clock had stopped at the exact
position where the second and the minute hands
overlap – but where do *we* come into all of this?

                    Listen to the ticking of my fingers
gaining words and losing time and even though
the fake flowers do not answer might I hear them:

                    how eternity is invisible
                    and fakeness is my state of mind

and if there's a metaphor in here somewhere
then the deductive proof is always in the reading.

v.

and then the sun?

I'd always wished for
then the sun
but completeness has a doubtful compactness to it
and all such elementary equivalence.

Beer for two in Brockler Park, Berlin

You asked me for a love poem
and I gave you a text message and a handful of
imaginary paprika crisps. You told me this was
insufficient to the moment and I agreed.
It was 3.08pm. I wrapped a single curl around
my index finger – smiled. *The thing about love
is the very thinginess of it. You must agree!
A 'now I've got you now I never won't'.*

I held the umbrella to your sunshine
the way you hold it to my rain: *tell me one thing
that I don't know about you?* We drank the beer,
confusing the order in which our books would've
liked the afternoon to turn around. *If I were you and
you were me* – I wondered – *might me marry you?*

III

Mine was a textbook response
to a century of abstract art
and the bleached paper on which I wrote
was neither nothing nor supreme.

> If concrete is not the opposite
> of abstract then it is the end of it –
> the most minimal of visual statements.

I out-stared the landscape's window
and forgave myself for everything.

i. Fin de siècle

at first i could barely even read
her nudité – excuse my French –
she was all angles and bones

the woman didn't even have a ticket
when she caught the bus
to the start of another century
and already running late
and the horse was motorised –

her lack of ticket changed perspective
and when I moved a metre to the right
the imitation of a woman disappeared entirely

ii. A hermetic landscape portrait

the self-sufficient hermit's spade
splits into fragments at the moment
it strikes the brittle earth

the passage of landscape travels through
the subject – on and by – but the young man
in the picture's apparent distraction
cannot be explained away so easily

the hermit turns the landscape in
upon himself:

if the earth is flat then antipathy
will be a ghastly mistake
and while a spade is no longer just a spade
just 40 cents will buy a fragment of a fragment
and associated accoutrements

(sticks and stones might break a poem
but words are more usually inserted)

iii. From the inside of a water lily out

blue oil falls
like thin pink water –

the unbearable humility
of lily floats vastness out
beyond the expectations
of a canvas page

       the immersive
       smallness
       of our inner gaze

       it had just been yet another
       little day

when the clock strikes six
the light of white departs
the willow's reflected reach upon
this most circular human stage –

iv. If the subject cannot count

take the pictorial equivalent
of how cubes curve towards
the natural dynamic impulse
of pure machine

or else
come here and – look!
come sit with life awhile

v. Towards Newton

The macabre booklover lies naked before the lotus
considering how money admires the condition of life.
This novelist has a way with silence and the women
in the local tavern. His is the song of man and the earth –
creation as a graduated motif of creation
with *this* chapter involving a portrait with someone else's wife.
I report the boudoir scene to the resistance.
The little girl with a ball has become a woman picking flowers
but victory is poor cover for equality.
Waves do not – and have not ever – cared for a sleeping face.

vi. Before time

When I was young and yet to lose my adolescent
heart and my eyes remained alight before
the already of everything I didn't know
I dreamt a polyglotic woman painted me

(clutterings
of someone else's memory entirely)

but my journey has long since slowed
and the train's decorative curtains can no longer
contain the excitable accents of a long past century.

I have sought to revisit every country
through the sound of colour –
yes that's me playing the piano –
I've been drunk for 500 kilometres of my life
already (sweet and quiet is the world asleep
but when I approach she steps away).

Ignorance has yet to forget
the ancient game of 'me' – these days
when I read about our cruelly illustrated world
is it to document myself?

Please accept the charge of my next memory
of the next day of my next-to-final voyage
and then might I sleep in my motley way.

vii. Me and the Moon

our evening was extracted
from the gravitational pull of a new moon
and a condition of minding each other's business

our unawareness caught us unaware
of how our own potential had been mapped
by the alpine heat-gradients of night –
the sky is alive with hues of clay-red and mustard
and the ground persists through varying intensities
of black – the condition of enforced absence

observe the post-abstracted domestic scene –
your voice contains cracked plaster
while my name is written in the smashed glass
of waning interference from the radio
that split the possibility of our combined future
from the surrounding view

viii. Composition

My primary aim in life is to learn to stroke
the surface of an unseen ocean.

The morning sun pierces the preceding horizon
like piccolo trumpet while the cobalt under-forest
squeezes dry onto the cluttered page.

I am waiting to fall (before too long)
into the angled living comfort of a stormy summer
under-sky – where rose-water undercoat exceeds

the softness of pure reference and the harsh black lines
of prehistoric birds and sabres and rearing horses
are remote from – how –

a living paen of praise, a hymn of new creation –
shapes that shadow what I cannot stand alone.

ix. Dynamism of a Speeding Horse + Houses

the past presents the simultaneous existence of a memory of new
perception introduced at considered speed: the x-ray of the horse-house
presented an illusion of the combustible duration of fast-copper-wood
and coated-iron cardboard transformed into the apparent dynamic
planes of unbound mortar floating shanks and open bone

x. Orthogonal

the late sunshine illuminated
the receding tide where a red fishing boat
just waited

the sea was horizontal
the fishing boat was looking for love
the sunshine was always moving elsewhere

xi. The wooden mannequin

And so I turn to turn from you:
a puppet with a small head and my personality
but a burden upon lifeless times.

> *Look!*
> (And look away again as soon as possible.)

How fast my short legs consume the spontaneous
combustion of air – a human mannequin is trying
to dance to poetry and when the dessicated earthflower
turns towards the sun – she asks you

                              did we really
                              and we *did* this?

If you'd only take a chance
then I'd do everything you tell me
in the most limited of imperfect ways.

xii. I am plant hammer

because the law of abstraction
is unfathomable as the primal
chance from which all life arises

                a spontaneous conception
apart   from the hand of:

                              I take a wooden hammer to
                              my final living houseplant
                              and I take a certain pleasure
                              from its absent cries

infinity is all over –
as complex as the form of organic relief

human immodesty is a form of self-hatred
and the container of meaning is overbrimming

                              if I call this art
                              and tell you
                              that I used to love you
                              will you please re-make me
                              in unreasonable order?

xiii. 5 x 5 = 25

The weasel is dead.
And all five living relatives contributed
a text for the handmade catalogue
of remembrance. The sanctity of
the weasel as a single entity has been
destroyed. We buried him in concrete
as a preparatory experiment but it didn't
taste so good.

Consciousness has become untenable,
and representation of weasels is over.

Our conclusion involves the unnecessary
multiplication of 25 individual weasel
lives – it is time to construct.

xiv. Cinema Dance Hall

Such new senses! Joy!
The stained glass windows
of this evening's programme
are filled with images of Man –
a hollow object which we use
to contain things in!

Their mouths are everyday
and their plastic bodies wear
the flattened planes of colours
of the universal style.

> *What are you here to see tonight,*
> *my friend? Or are you dancing?*

The diners are climbing up the ceilings
and the hors d'oeuvre will soon come to float
in space and we won't consider this unusual.

Time is moving in the heretical diagonal.
Can you feel the tension in the room?
May I introduce myself as (no less than)
the inventor of the lozenge.

xv. Redesigning the building house

Before painting
came the theory of painting
and craft might be a fine thing.

The early days of colour arose from the form
of wood plus stone and to be 'at one' with yourself
was a question for the design of loose
first principles.

Nature remains an elemental material of basic space
but to have a spirit inevitably involves machines –
the machine possessed all slaves and the streamlined
human blueprint was ordered in by telephone.

> The impersonality of the lightbulb is complete –
> turn your eye to anything that becomes available.
> I had meant to write a poem and I built a bridge from it.

xvi. Bird in Space

What's the taxable rate of paper per poem?
The gorgeous bird caught a fish and ate it
from its pedestal of a large river stone.

(Excuse my lack of detail
no furore lacks intention.)

The bird was made of metal and the fish
was executed
simply and characteristically.

xvii. The Birth of the World

our world began with a random gesture
marked upon the margins of the sky
with a single horizontal back-splash
of a painter's life

the sun and moon came later
and the people grew from sticks and our
brains became the matter
of coalescing storm clouds

a backless spine holds tight to the winding
skyward trajectory of some accidental sperm
as the upturned plough speeds west

the dots join the lines and as the weather
trickles from the page your big toe stands on
a spider but your imagination holds firm –

the lack of colour is a reproductive after-
thought of how the legless spider got away

xviii. Morning Henri

Because I found God
I lost my body
and because my body was lost
I had more space in the morning.

To exist is to change,
to change is to mature,
to mature is to go on creating oneself endlessly.

Which is all very well,
but where's my coffee, Henri?

xix. *It's all over the city*

You have three choices ahead of you
and none of them are yours.

1. It's all over – the city extends
its tentacles across the surrounding landscape
like a huge orgasm on a drunken boat.

2. It's all over the city. The happy couple
massage each other's feet inside the pagoda
known locally as the pavilion of elegance
in such a breathingly human way that I somehow
come to dream of blue phantoms and butterfly
wings. The universal horror of being-in-the-world
and other things.

3. It's all. Over the city descended a strange kind
of otherness. It was as if we were suddenly inhabiting
a cave, and our words were made of radio, and the rock
which might guard the entrance to the city was out of reach.
I've always been a blue kind of an optimist. Untitled.
Scarred as a windmill sketch.

xx. *At the edge of August*

at the edge of August
I found letters – an unknown script –

the light already felt tired
of feeling tired
and I could feel my writing slipping
towards the dark

           the earth's tongue
is pink and slantwise
and while I did not do
I thought about it –

all the words I'd heard
that year cocooned my brain
like loosely woven silk-trippings

xxi. Of texturology

The soil teemed with itself:
the sparkling nebulae of
the indeterminacy of matter
might evoke galaxies

and even an impression of
kindness. The texture of the
representation of the exemplary
state of being alive.

The abstract earth breaks down
the material beauty of ugliness.
A painter enacts our smallness
upon the scattered floor.

xxii. Homage

because every perception
of words is an illusion
we do not hear words
the way they really are:

how ace
becomes lace
becomes place
becomes replaced
by the irreplaceable act
of the very opposite of itself

you see – the way
the words have lifted off the surface
of the page

xxiii. Full Fathom Five

ice
broken and dripping

> this is the epic
> of undone
> total ocean

> a young man turns his pockets out
of nails
tacks
buttons
coins and cigarettes

while the turquoise ocean dances with sand
and the weather skeins towards
the centre of itself and back again
and I'm holding firmly on to yellow
as if art depends on it

> you ask me if I like it and I agree
> because actions cannot speak but words do?

the painting is somehow louder
than I anticipated, in its quietest of ways –

> thick brushed strokes and the detritus
> of ice-break pouring

> so hark! now tell me if you hear them!

I don't know why you chose this point
to ask me what I thought about the future

xxiv. Painting

meanwhile, out west,
we are committed to an unqualified act
apart

there is no such thing as broad darkness
until the moment that we enter into it

xxv. Untitled / and dancing

Today I am working on the scenic design
of interior landscape and mainly trying
not to watch you dancing.

Never before have I realised the potential
in the texture of a cufflink
nor the ambiguity of the condensation
in the corner of a bathroom window
illuminated by late evening light.

You continue dancing.
Is there not such possibility in the reflection
of a stone caught floating downstream
or in the oriental patterns of your palm
simplified to a calligraphic black on white?

If I wrote about you
then you'd soon enough complain
about the rough impasto of my words.

There is no beauty but detail: the work
of the world is rough and uncompleting
and its refusals just keep flowing from you.

xxvi. Seagram

sit – not too close – to the sea
or you will fail to see
how the tide has become embroiled
in the gannets' vertical melancholy

> one fish
> two fishes
> (many is just another
> way to express a very few)

I hold a rough wooden frame
to the sky and watch
the birds pierce the surface of the sea
and the claret fractus clouds
scudding from view.

There are only seven seasons and
I've already painted thirty of them.

xxvii. Onement

Just look at this face
and tell me. Is this not a happy face?

The old woman's smile reaches
beyond the edges of her head –
stolen by the undergrowth into the park bushes
and on. Her anorak is zipped up absolutely
to her chin and the Jack Russell at her feet
is looking a little formless / gormless.
Predominantly ochre. As if he wasn't really
a Jack Russell or a dog at all.

She hands a stolen biscuit to her ochre non-dog
and turns her chin towards a chink

of the November sun. *Imagine that!*
Will you ever listen to the biscuit barking?

My sense of overall atonement is (how to put it)
just / wonderful. I decide to describe the scene
despite myself as – *pleasing* – as if pleasure
were a problem for another day and all –

xxviii. Reflections on the materiality of abstraction

the diagonal shafts of light across the vast sheet of stainless steel
make me reflect upon the matter of potential

> hope is a big word
> in small concrete form

I cut it into planes and bars and pieces and recombine
the possibility of open metal space

xxix. White Field

the experimental farmer
planted twenty thousand wooden poles
and waited for the sky to grow

he was not to be
disappointed

xxx. Blue

It is impossible to size the summer sky
and you will always fail in your attempts
to estimate the total quantity of sea.

If green is for grass
then dark red is my rusty deux-chevaux
and light cream is the happy colour
of my matching kettle and toaster set
which I recently replaced from the internet
just down the road.

(Indeed is a fine word
and I try to utilise it frequently.)

In my first experiment I made my brain
more tangible. In my second test
I calculated the formula of failure.
My woollen jumper is a lovely jumper,
you'd agree. It is silent. It is blue.

xxxi. Alphabet

The contrast between our alphabets
might bear witness to violence
but I remain neutral –

the world is but a chessboard
construction of steel and zinc
and we've lost the players
to their individual alphabets already.

There is no one place
where you should be.
And I am nobody
you know
and this the final ladder to the final sky.

The world was better before
I cut it
than it turned out afterwards –
I promise not to improve the world in any way.

xxxii. *Plight*

The story of the piano involves the intricate set
of possibilities it offers up to me –
when the child was born they swaddled him
in fat and felt and lay him on a grand piano
and the Tatars sang pentatonic songs to him.
Our current plight relates to the right way
to play a Bach fugue for consumption
by a middle-class Sunday-afternoon audience.

The baby smells of museum. The piano is
unconscious of the precise angle of its placement
on the parquet floor. The musicality of the
overwhelming ambiance absorbs you. When I'm
older I'm going to consider the many possibilities
that I might have been. Like a piano. Like a child, even.

xxxiii. *Neo–untitled*

something borrowed:
you reduce me and reduce me
and reproduce me

xxxiv. *The figurative abstract*

behind you lies the distillation
of twenty-four hours of thin air –
a century of art and a month
of touching on the unfinality
of reappearance

> I keep on hearing isolated
> bits of conversation –
> perhaps from dreams –
> perhaps from any number
> of the paintings which have come before

you said that you were made of
house and garden and ocean and sky
but I particularly enjoyed your lack of
explanation for the way the trees are hiding
from the hill

you've taught me – that there are many shades
of triangle and the deconstruction of an empty
swimming pool and a statue of a urinating boy is
always in the detail

but myself I've never been so good
at endings – see?

listen to the laughter of a rhapsodic horde
of swimmers in the near-off distance
close your eyes and if you like
the nothing you can see please call me

The poems in this sequence are responses to the following paintings / groupings and the 'poetics' informing them:

i.   Pablo Picasso, 'A Female Nude'
ii.   Georges Braque, 'Le Portugais'
iii.   Claude Monet, 'Water Lilies'
iv.   Fernand Léger, 'Contrasting Forms'
v.   Frantisek Kupka, 'Disks of Newton'
vi.   Sonia Delauney, various
vii.   Arthur Dove, 'Me and the Moon'
viii.   Wassily Kandinsky, 'Composition IV'
ix.   Umberto Boccioni, 'Dynamism of a Speeding Horse + Houses'
x.   Piet Mondrian, *Pier and Ocean* series
xi.   Sophie Taueber, various
xii.   Hans Arp, 'Plant Hammer'
xiii.   After the 5x5 exhibition involving Rodchenko, Ekster, Popova, Stepanova & Vesnin
xiv.   Van Doesburg, Interior of the Café d'Aubette, Cinema Dance Hall
xv.   László Noholoy-Magy at the Bauhaus
xvi.   Constantin Brancusi, 'Bird in Space'
xvii.   Joan Miró, 'The Birth of the World'
xviii. Alfred Manessier, 'Morning Space'
xix.   Wols, 'It's all over – the city'
xx.   Mark Tobey, 'Edge of August'
xxi.   Jean Dubuffet, 'Texturology'
xxii.   Josef Albers, 'Homage to the Square'
xxiii. Jackson Pollock, 'Full Fathom Five'
xxiv.   Clyfford Still, 'Painting'
xxv.   Franz Kline, various
xxvi.   Mark Rothko, 'Seagram'
xxvii. Barnett Newman, 'Onement III'
xxviii. David Smith, '8 Planes and 7 Bars'
xxix.   Gunther Uecker, 'White Field'
xxx.   Yves Klein, various
xxxi.   Carl Andre, various
xxxii. Joseph Beuys, 'Plight'
xxxiii. Sherri Levine, 'Untitled'
xxxiv. Jennifer Bartlett, various

IV

The canal guillotine appeals to its reflection
as if the watercolour of its final hours might
finally appease the small-mapping of history –

what history?

The student of the world is introduced to
the subtlety involved in being an artefact.
Alive with all that implies. Without relevance.

Apropos of nothing

The rain made the rainbow
because art has no colour
and you can more likely
run your hands through a fool
than you will ever discover gold.

Mine was the last watch
before the apocalypse ended
and even my fear was almost over:

what's a raindrop that's not
a raindrop truth be told?

I would show you my hand
if I had a hand and I would ask you
to read my palm if I had a palm
and I would show you a mirror
if you were really there.

I remember this slightly foreign phrase
my mother used to use and I lie
it here – beside me – on the pre-existent earth.

Now count to ten and open your eyes
and tell me the colour of the weather.

Me and my sister

My gran still wrings the neck
of the pre-plucked chook that flew away
and my mother nearly dying.

> *She is only young, grandmother,*
> *and cannot know much better.*

I have been bad, and was here, to be there,
not far from home, only three years old,
three miles from home and the sudden
all-consuming noise has just created   (silence).

I'm lying in a white bed bigger than my unformed
knowledge of death while my mother has become
the inverse of herself – wearing all her organs
from the outside in. We are already stationary.
There is a knocking on the window.
There is a child in the back. I cannot breathe.
It is dark, and somebody is knocking at the window
and the most awful noise has just created silence.
There is a child in the back and I cannot breathe
and then was nothing, then, but nothing.

The steering wheel has been embedded in the future
of my mother's spine. We are stopped. I am alone.
It is black and white and long and I must forget
the way the car bonnet cut through my mother's line of sight.

> *I cried and cried, but still you did not answer me.*

My gran still wrings the neck of the pre-plucked chook
that flew away and the noise was awful. I must have been
so bad, but *she is young, grandmother,* a*nd cannot know much better.*

Where is winter?

Winter has been elsewhere. Winter crept up
on the snowman when he wasn't looking and threw
pebbles and carrots at him. Winter sometimes wears
stars on its sky like a glittered bauble. Winter has hidden
in the soles of my feet and the inverse of my eyes.
Perhaps my sister borrowed winter for her
imaginary underworld and made it speak funny.
Winter gave my hat to the leafy gutter.
I said 'what are you trying to prove, winter?'
but it did not stop to listen. Because winter is pumped
full of weather and darkness. If you lit a match
to winter it would not burn. Winter evades me:
winter is the I of the storm, and the beholder
has long since wrapped up warm as hats and gloves.

Antarctic skies

the day the clouds became rainbows
the fishing boat turned a blind eye to the sea
and pursued its futility of dreams

the fishing boat hadn't always wanted
to travel to the stratosphere upon a wave
of iridescent sky – this was a new thing
among fishing boats and all the better for it –

the fishing boat floated to the place
where the sky-sea has such holes that boats
fall through your mind like coloured migraines
and fish outsource the sabre moon

by the time that night had fallen
there was no atmosphere to speak of
but a host of silent stars –

I could not own my cut of such futility
but catching on to it –

the summer that the adolescence policemen
knocked upon my door I swam the river out the back
door to the sea and stole the last remaining
fishing boat from the sea-bed's sky of stone

Although the visitants wore fedoras

the world is a clod of earth in space
the cake is yellow
and the sky stands tall –

my mother warned me about the texture
of the internet and the paleness of water
but i did not listen –

listening is a trick you hide
behind doors and sometimes talk about –

before you know it yesterday becomes
an apology for everything to come
while the future lives on deep inside your bones

    what's your name
    and are you welcome here?

the cat sat on your hat
the fedora fell over the nose of a rain storm
into your teacup and you should have heard
my mother scream then

    but still you wore
    the day away with all your questions

that night the kitchen had little to do
with anything apart from the relative size
of cake-tins to the stage of the cyber-moon

Sotto voce

I took the day our words left shore
for a place less unknown
than known and followed it.

I was not afraid of adulthood
as such yet certain of it.

The waves already followed the rhythm
of a pattern of thought
which was not mine – nor ours?

They always talked of progress
yet the sky endured so vast and changing
that I couldn't even tell if we were moving.

The salt-encrusted plank of wood
I travelled on was but a solitary comfort –

just wearing out more driftwood poems
from an aversion to an emotion
I was not large enough – nor still –
to contain nor say.

Application to be a war artist

after Hans Arp

I am pregnant with shells and driftwood
strung together with wire and suspended
from my oesophagus with a fishing buoy head.

I have lifted off the surface of the universe
and while its skin of planet and star and sky
peels free, I'm floating west and east and south
upon the breeze –

> My name is Jean
> My name is Hans
> My name is Lucy

I truly have no name and I've scrawled
it illegibly on each and every space
of your application page.

I remove my clothes –
please use your imagination, and tell me everything
you do not see.

I am pregnant with shells and driftwood
strung together with wire and suspended
from my oesophagus with a fishing buoy head.
Your cold concretion is as sensuous as a leaf.

Ben Hope – a direct plebiscite

Did you hear the one about
the itinerant snail in search of home?

I rewind my adulthood some years:
retuning the dreich burr of the early morning news
to a sense more akin to relief than I tend to feel these days

> (when the snail awoke the ayes had voted
> its leaf abroad?)

I hesitate to speak of what I couldn't choose
and would have chosen
and there's an easy kind of familiarity to this
that puts me ill at ease.

I happened to be born
on the patchy side of a northern Roman wall
we learnt about at football matches more than
school:

> *stand up if you hate…!*

> I am neither aye nor no
> but there's something other in it
> somehow than the game the upstanding
> supporters failed to see.

I stand on the summit of the northernmost hill
in Scotland and I start to dance –
d'you mind the time they tried to sell the mountains?

Tomorrow – meanwhile – beyond the patchy wall
where I've paused to make a home far south of home
the world is being moved.

My fortune – until now –
consists in rarely having woken up afraid.

Painterly Realism of a Football Player

after Kasimir Malevich

The non-existent stadium hangs suspended
from the abyss of outer space and I'm straddling
the boundary of the pitch's near horizon.

The earth keeps tripping over gravity
and the sun has fallen from the sea
and *I've* fallen so in love with shadows as of late

that the green football disappears against the grass
and the linesman sends a semaphore
and the crowd begins to shout *the referee's a wanker.*

    Come after me, comrade aviators, sail into the chasm.

I am a colour metaphor that came from nothing.
The beyond horizon beckons, infinite as
the canvas which I empty of every little corner of things.
I came from nothing comrade – and *I'm* with red.

The brexfast after

refilling the bitter smell
of the first morning coffee
with something more akin to fear
than I like to
acknowledge these days

there are two options
ahead of you – take your pick!
but I honestly cannot
tell you what they are

       1. show me your palm –
       let me erase your future

       2. what does it even *mean*
       to lie these days
       and will you agree
       that it is easily done
       and in the initial stages
       comparatively painless too

       3. I am looking out of the window
       and I do not recognise
       the familiar smell of changeable weather
       and even though this option is not available
       I hope it rains –

do you know?
I did not ask for my own opinion
and you spoke above me
until I shared your shame

tomorrow is another day –
I fear – and yesterday's coffee
not yet begun

The birds still singing

I had never – exactly – disliked
red bricks – but they had not as yet
become me

but that day
I said fuck the terraces of brick
and the over-eaten grass
and the arrangement of the view
and the interminable
dislike of the weather

and I said fuck
the skin-head surface of the estate
and the exaggerated drone
of souped-up exhaust fumes
calling us to prayer

(and these are not *whose* jobs
or I might have listened)

and especially –
I say fuck to the underhand way
I launch a red brick through
the window of a very pleasant Sunday dinner
of another very pleasant Sunday home

I stop – apologise

Here I am at the centre
of a very pretty island alone
and the nearby conversation cutting borders
from my sides

I am the brick becomes me
and the birds still singing

Despite the negative press covfefe

in response to a Twitter post from Donald Trump on 31 May 2017

Meaning   that having spent the morning
watching TV news and thinking
about the incessant angle
of all the past six months'
November rain – that to be lost
for words becomes a form of
surroundment

    language meeting its date of definition
at the point of introduction / identity:

            OPTIONS
            RETURN
            GUIDE
            HOME

      the synchronised channel-hopping
of the remote-controlled political rain beads upon
the Velux window like oil
off the tongues of quite so many commentators

    observe the minute differences
        of allusion – emulsion – elusion –
for I could not repeat to you a word they said

    but to trust is conditional
    and to lie is a parallel of truth
    and to speak bigly equates to the hope
    that tomorrow really never comes?

    the weather dial has lost its patience with
the sudden loss of sunlight –
a falling liquid time-thread
slips   and sleeks   and runs   then goes

The dripping tap

I know one thing.

A handshake
is more orange than a bullet
and a Stetson is a large dog.

I once met a woman
crying about America.

The necessity of the intellect

after Wassily Kandinsky

1. What is your first reaction to the triangle?
2. How would you rate the quality of blue?
3. How innovative is this movement to the left? (Does it leave you feeling cold or warm?)
4. When you think about this painting, do you think of it as something that you need or do not need?
5. How would you rate the value for money of visual dissonance?
6. If this palette were available today, how likely would you be to buy it?
7. How likely are you to replace your emotions for your mind?
8. How likely is it that you would recommend this universal law to your friends?
9. In your own words, what do you see of yourself in this painting?
10. In your own words, what would you most like to abstract from improved art?

The flight of the guillemet

Chapter 1

‹There is something not quite right about Guillaume. Guillaume knows the feel of paper the way that birds navigate the sky. What came first the guillemet or the empty page? Guillaume wears red slippers and a balding black toupée. Guillaume will come and find you. Guillaume has stolen your dictionary and is making origami from it. Some things have come to be expected from Guillaume›

Chapter 2

‹When Guillame removes a book from the library he incurs a future risk: in case there are no facts no matter how inventive he might be. He has observed journalists peter out from the brink of their addiction to the smell of fresh print. After all, there does not seem to be a law of human nature. If Guillaume indexed the alternative truth then he would find it a simple exercise, but he would be unlikely to tell you why›

Chapter 3

‹Guillaume knows that there are many things far worse for your health than smokers – *go and see the foundations of sand upon which we built this exercise for your own eyes*! Guillaume keeps on making memories that he can't let lie, and dreams that even the court of law finds sleep elusive. Guillaume likes to think that he is trending as an interpretation of the current historic paradigm: *it is normal for one or two arguments to have been born dead!* But no matter how *young* Guillaume feels, the facts undoubtedly slow down as he gets older›

Chapter 4

‹Guillaume suspects that there is no apparent cause for older people – *how common are they?* He stretches out his arms until the pain begins to ease: the aim of the exercise is to loosen up your doctor. Guillame has come to find life most painful first thing in the morning. He is prepared for disappointment. *Can old age be prevented by simply talking to oneself?*>

The thing about eggs

Imagine that you have no name. I had woken
before my alarm and lay staring into my eyelids
for a good half hour.
If you were a poem, what would you be most
frightened of? Brown paper bags. Sonnets.
I've got this thing about coagulated egg.
Outside my kitchen window the day begins.
The sky is grey. Nothing rhymes with egg.

Or imagine you have a name. Some things never
change, but this isn't one of them. A single
teaspoon lies on the table. I like brown paper bags
but there is no such a thing as a happy sonnet.
Take the example of eyes or eggs. The thing about
names is the way they wobble and they look at you.

De-named

only notes of privilege
a kind of terror
and saying

I confess
I cannot
imagine

upon the strike of war
the air exploding,

Mouvements

after Henri Michaux

The lace lamp in advanced flight
resembles the overflow unit of a dance block
as the disappeared eventually disappears –
we are connected more than ever.

Man. Man jump. Men's man.
A man for the blitz in boyband practice
creating harpoons by studying the ripping
operation of sharks.

After it is meat, it is no longer human being,
but – according to the sky and evil – internal flame
that flashes the discharge nerve, dissatisfied,
and returns in anger.
No people. Meat satisfaction is impossible.

But what a debut!
Another year according to gust and chaos.
I have never ordered man –
a man is not sealed nor cultivated.

·

Until this humiliating life, I wished to be present.
The sound of a cymbal, pierce drill, stamp teenager.
I am a woman, yet
I do not understand what breasts mean –
rumours – they increase the blood tide through the heart
until suddenly in an artery, we change direction.

Thirst. Especially thirst.
But I do not have any thirst.

The eyelash of my soul is draped in algae.
The electrification of a larval core. I bite the surface.
Did you hear the knock of the soul-tooth?
Always a door with a wrong soul.

I extend in all directions and refuse
what unhealthy attraction requests of me.
I will beat my neck with no head movement.

I saw my soul but we cannot display it.
Dust, star-erosion, mudslide. Unnecessary standby
time in the range of my behaviour or an exercise
in walking.

                    I will go –
                              But I will go to what?

                              •

We are a crowd of many progresses
and a lie. A lie will be added. Adieu fatigue.
Efficient walking of the biped in the early state.
Pillar, torn sheath. This is another existence.

Any weakness, any geometry, and all architectures.
Abstraction makes speed!
Take the example of this open flower arrangement
without the benefit of line for context!

But we have a stride now. It's called hope –
the height of a jump in thought.
It has eight legs whether it works or not.
Sometimes it is rooted. That is to hold it.
We have never been beaten, and we always return again.

Cryptic

v. the act of preferring the questions to the answers

So here I am again, once more lost for morning,
wearing the kind of clothes that the French might wear
to attend class (as a means of embellishing a new day
by the sounds of it).

No, I am not the full amount, you tell me,
with the confidence of a referee with a famous mother.
I am but a brassica stalk for a king – a place from which
to observe the prospect of a transplanted tree.

It is very true, you will find me in a disturbed state.
My social status will more than likely produce a row –
but underneath it all, I am a flower opening out near the sea!
The fragrance of a European flower, it has been said.

When you last turned up, you were surrounded by
an unusually deadly volatile fluid. But your uniform chant
for the service was poor criteria as far as the flag officers
were concerned (you'd been fed up and it came right back

again). Our conversation was a little like a stringed
instrument received in acclamation, perhaps, describing
the great range of an ecclesiastic! Ok, so they are downtrodden
in-flight, not to put down the expenditure.

So here I am, in a casualty station more commonly
used by sportsmen. My business has combined
to produce mulled claret used for bringing fish to shore.
I like going out. I like a night to remember.

I would like to be a solid container that increases
sonority. Am I trusting my instincts to your affairs?
Unlikely – you will find me in a disturbed state,
guiding into target and returning to base.

Dead time

So *this* stone marks the place of the house that Jack built.
The stone has two ears and a nose and an eye in the middle
of its forehead – just like Jack. The stone bears the stones of other houses –
mottled as a concrete mongrel. Grass invades the crevices of its
pitted-pebbled scalp and that mouldy smell of long-gone summer.

Remember?

This stone is from the house that marks the place that Jack built.
Dead as this Jack is the house the stone killed.
Dead as this Jack is the weight of the stone's guilt,
is the possibility that Jack and the house and the stone once filled.

The Electric Press

Millennium Square, Leeds, 2018

The golden owl turns its neck from the pub
and stares illness in the face,
while two pigeons puff their heads deep into their chests
and four commuters rush across the concrete –
not even pausing to think about thinking.

When the millennium failed to realise
its own ending, and the computers just went ahead
and changed, and I was climbing the beer-spattered struts
of Jabob's Ladder to watch the New Year fireworks
in a knee-length leopard skin coat and nylon orange flares,
then where were *you* (and was I truly looking marvellous)?

> (And where *were* you when a car crashed into
> the Bridge of Souls, and I was falling in and out
> of love, and fairly simultaneously?
>
> On which floor of what building were you
> standing when the second plane 'hit', and I
> half-watched an unlikely visual film plot on the TV
> of a campsite bungalow bar in rural Wales, while
> playing pool? *But it's not a film love. It's life.*)

Perhaps it's *you* I'm watching, on the large screen backdrop
to the closure of this afternoon. You're wearing a grey hooded
tracksuit and hiding from the rolling credits of the life you've
spent the past hour wasting. An empty wine glass on a table
from the café down below pretends it's summer.

The clock reads 5.08pm. The wind is westerly, it's cold out,
but the sun is palely shining. And while the ELECTRIC PRESS
props up the cumulus, the townhall pillars rest securely
upon the neck-extension of a security guard's muscled spine

(if there really is a bunker under here, I'd hope to be
included on the wartime guest list for wine and canapés!)

I've got this thing about the instant –
when now becomes the future.

Most of all –
I'd like to be that workman erecting scaffolding
for the something that might happen, if we're lucky, later on.

Big Friday

Vafes, Crete

If I were a mountain
I would offer you
thyme   and time   again

for it's yet late
and the morning and the sunshine hold me
where the breeze shares air with scarred scree

      (it's been so long and my snow
      – still barely – melting)

can you taste the springtime fragrance of un-named
flowers and unseen birdsong?

Down-hill-wind a single gunshot fires the death of winter
while the bells are chiming twice for every hour
and children march a scarecrow through the village streets
shouting words I wasn't born to and haven't learnt
to understand.

      You extend your kindly invitation to observe
a ritual of belief
I've never shared and I prevaricate –

      history is marching slowly
      to the graveyard.

A cross marks the summit where the time of year is easing
and I believe in sea and sky and the bell-ringing of goats
and the scalpelled edge of rock on snow
and if you care to turn towards me even
in this dead of springtime you will find me –

Of the roses

nothing wished to say
in abundance

not my story taken
by way of the old drove roads

> i have been alone
> since middle england
> and truth telling on me –

> so many – much – lies
> beneath the oneiric surface –

> the white of an unbleached rose
> flows from crimson red
> and back again

but what of it – if nothing?

I'm no stranger
to unfamiliar eyes –

I've been living at the edges of earth
for what might seem centuries

> (the world is neither
up nor down but other)

but if somewhere beyond
the accepted line of place / time –
an amorphous flower is beckoning

– there once was a golden sign –
abstract unstalked unproper